The Journey

Finding Healing through Scripture from Life's Hard Questions

By using Scripture and
the "Coach Approach,"
you will start the journey to healing &
understanding.

The Coach Approach Workbook
for Small Groups or Individuals
by
Rhonda Gould, CPLC, ACC

The Journey: Finding Healing through Scripture from Life's Hard Questions

by: Rhonda Gould, CPLC, ACC

Coloring pages created in full by Rhonda Gould of Rhonda Gould Coaching & Consulting

ISBN: 979-8-218-02556-4

Printed by Ingram Sparks Publishing, Inc. in the United States of America

First printing, August 2022

Cover Photo by Canva.com

Scripture quotations are from various versions of the Holy Bible using BibleGateway.com

Rhonda Gould, CPLC, ACC, Winchester, KY

Contact information for Rhonda Gould through www.rhondagouldonline.com.

For a FREE coaching session go to: rhondagouldonline.com/contact-for-free-initial-session/

Table of Contents

Want ANSWERS?

A – Ask Him

N – Need Him

S – Seek Him

W – Woo You

E – Encourage You

R – Reveal to You

S – Save You

James 1:5-6 If any of you lacks wisdom, you should ask God, who gives generously to all without finding fault, and it will be given to you.

But when you ask, you must believe and not doubt, because the one who doubts is like a wave of the sea, blown and tossed by the wind.

Dedication

To those who have questions about life.

Acknowledgment

My Family, Tom, Sawyer, Shaine, Jennifer, and Summer. You are the best family that I could ask for. We have learned to trust in God together. There have been some tough times, but also some joyous times. I am grateful that you have stuck by me through them all. You have shown me love, grace, and unconditional mercy. To my husband, Tom, you are my rock. To our sons, Sawyer & Shaine, my supportive daughters-in-law, Jennifer and Summer, and our five beautiful grandchildren, I love you more than I could even express.

Carol Stewart, you are the one person that invested in me in the most important way, by sharing Jesus with me. Your life is a living example to me of what service and love looks like. I am forever grateful to you and love you bunches.

Rachel Solomon & Sandy H. Malsom, for 35 years you have poured into me with a love that could only come from your deep and constant love of God. You have been my confidants, my shoulders, my encouragers, my mentors, and my second moms. Rachel, I wish I had followed the calling of authoring this book before you went to Heaven, but I am positive you are cheering me on from above just as you did when I first started this journey. Sandy, you will be the first to cheer me on and encourage me here on earth. I am grateful that you will get to see this book come to fruition. Your love and consistent care has kept me going.

Jenny Newberry & Teresa Moran, I have mentioned your names to so many because you encouraged me to step out of my comfort zone so many years ago. You believed "I could do it," which increased my trust in God and allowed me to grow and be courageous for HIM.

The Big 5- Amy Baradell, Angela Schlentz, Melanie H. Clayton, Susan Creed, & Pamela Slepp, we have been through it together. No matter what has happened, you have been by my side unconditionally through thirty-five years of spurring each other on, calling each other out, and holding each other up. Thank you for every loving, encouraging word.

Friends, there have been so many people who have played a vital role in helping me walk this life. You know who you are! Love you!

Remember, it is the little words that make the biggest impact!

Enjoy doing a little coloring throughout the process to give your heart & mind a break from what can be heavy.

Introduction

Life can be hard and messy. I have learned that you cannot get past your past unless you face it head-on. I hope that by sharing bits and pieces of my past, you will see that while I continue to face the struggles of life, I am also able to find joy. I pray that you will be able to share in my experiences to find connection and comfort, which will then lead to healing through the process that I have laid out.

Many years ago, after some very intentional steps of picking up the pieces of my life, I knew God was telling me to author a book. I did not know what that would look like, but I spoke the words many times. As I am constantly reminded by the things I have learned in life, I have also learned that God's timing is perfect. I may not always understand it, but I trust it. It is His time.

This book comes from my heart. A heart that is full of pain but overflows with JOY. He has done that for me. He has always shown me that HE has a better plan. He has always carried me through the storms of life and landed me back on my feet. Without Him, I would be lost.

Jesus exemplified the principle of prayer in what we identify as the *Lord's Prayer.* For that reason, I have included it in each step.

Our Father, who art in Heaven, hallowed by Thy Name. Thy Kingdom come, Thy will be done on earth, as it is in heaven. Give us this day our daily bread. And forgive us our debts, as we forgive our debtors. And lead us not into temptation. But deliver us from evil. For thine is the kingdom, the power, and the glory, forever and ever Amen.

Prayer is vital to finding answers. A true and deep relationship with the Lord is our only hope. Without prayer, it is impossible to have that relationship. Our relationship with the Lord is like any other relationship. Without dialogue, there is nothing. Can you imagine going through life without speaking to your spouse or closest friend? How would you both be able to communicate your needs, desires, and frustrations? How would you share your love with them? How would they know your heart? It is simple; they would not.

I know there have been times when I did not have the words to accurately express how I was feeling at the time. The Bible says that God sent the Holy Spirit to comfort us and intercede on our behalf when we have no words. Through prayer, He will know your heart. He will hear you.

I grew up an only child, and it was only me and my mom until I was six years old. I thought that was normal. As a child, I was happy and felt loved. My mom married my stepfather when I was six, and we moved to a neighboring town, where I started school, made friends, and loved being a child. I remember wanting a sister and begging for them to have a baby. The day came when my mom got pregnant, and I was so excited. I was not going to be alone in this world any longer. Until that dreaded day came.

When my teacher called me out of class, I knew something was terribly wrong. I hear the words, "your mom has been in a car accident and is being taken to the hospital." As a child, I was not sure how to process the information. Was she okay? Is my sister that I have been waiting for, okay? I went home with my best friend and after some time, I hear that they both will be okay. At almost nine, I also believed that life would go back to what I knew as "normal," and we all would be okay. But it did not, and we were not! This newly turned nine-year-old now was thrusted into the role of caregiver to my baby sister. Pain for mom was at times too much because of her injuries so the household responsibilities also became part of my day-to-day life. Our whole family had a new normal!

The biggest and most difficult change I experienced was still to come. Shortly after the birth of my sister, I experienced a violation that no child should endure. The violation was "childhood sexual abuse." I can still vividly account the times, places, and what the violator said. Actions and words that I now know to be forms of "grooming." This continued for many years, and I believed others expected this of me, so I put my head down and kept going. Even after the abuse ended physically, it never left me mentally or emotionally. Little did I know at the time, but I brought that belief into my everyday life as a child, teenager and it followed me into my marriage. This belief brought with it endless shame, guilt, confusion, and a lack of self-worth. This has been the baggage I have carried for my whole life. This is what was in my closet. This is the secret that has haunted me and guided most of my decisions until the day I decided to face it forty-plus years later.

Sometimes I wonder how I made it through those years and still came out in decent shape. I did not know God at the time. I did not have anyone I could tell. I had no one in my corner. So, it just followed me. And at times, I was lonely. As an adult, I began the journey with Jesus and was learning all about His love for me and how He provides, protects, and redeems me. However, for the first thirty or so years of following Jesus, there was a huge part of me still hiding in the closet with my dirty little secret. I convinced myself I was dealing with it just fine. I did not want or see the need to face it and then I found the reason, "someone I loved" was my reason.

That brings me to today, authoring a book to help you on your question-filled journey. Our questions about our past and/or current situations will vary in as many ways as the leaves blow in the wind. There is only one sure way to get the answers to those questions, and that is to go to God through His word. Seeking out what His word says about what we discover through the process is our only hope for healing. God will bring healing to the broken-hearted.

I have authored this book exposing every fiber of my heart and earnestly praying for healing. Please take your time working through these steps. Do not rush the process or you will miss His message. Dig deep into the meaning and reason for your questions. Explore the why of your questions and seek awareness that you may not have even thought about. Doing this will help the healing process begin. You will see the reason for your questions. You will be able to find answers. If you do not feel some of the steps fit into the questions that you have raised, then sit on it for a while and see what HE may bring to your mind. Do not shy away from looking into the hard places of your soul because it feels dark there. The only way to break out of the darkness is to open the door to that closet and let God's light shine into your soul. Let Him in. He is for you. He loves you. He wants you to seek Him, and He will be with you in every step that you take as long as you invite Him. He will not force you, but He desperately longs for you to be in a relationship with Him. Ask Him in, welcome Him in and lean on His truth. How much do you want healing? What are you willing to sacrifice to find healing? What would it mean to you to have healing? When will you be ready to start healing?

Pray with me: *Lord, I pray that I will look to you and your words to heal my weary and broken heart. Give me the strength and the courage to take the steps I need to find healing through you. Give me comfort and peace through the process and bring awareness about how much you love me. Amen.*

Types of questions that I had to process are.....

What would God have me do with my past?

How do I know it is God speaking to me?

What is God's purpose for me?

What does forgiveness look like when reconciliation is not possible?

Journey Quotes:

"A lie can travel halfway around the world while the truth is putting on its shoes." - Unknown

"Before you judge my life, my past, or my character. walk in my shoes, walk the path I have traveled, live my sorrow, my doubts, my fear, my pain, and my laughter." - Unknown

"I still have my feet on the ground, I just wear better shoes." - Unknown

"We all walk in different shoes."- Kenneth Cole

"Yours are the only shoes made to walk your journey." – Charles F. Glassman

Understanding the Journey Process

This workbook is a journey of how I have learned to find the answers to extremely tough questions about life. I have not wavered in my trust in His plan. I am inviting you to embark on a Joy-filled life by taking a journey with God. Discover how to navigate through Life's Hard Questions by diving deep into yourself and scripture which will lead you to find answers, healing, and a closer relationship with God.

A journey according to webster's dictionary is an act of traveling from one place to another. A physical journey in car or plane can lead you to turns, winding roads, and many obstacles. Our physical or even emotional journeys are the same. We can encounter many obstacles or stumbling blocks that can cause us to reconsider our paths, stop us all together, tell ourselves lies, and make hasty decisions. There are issues and joys on our journey.

Learning how to navigate through our journey can be challenging without guidance from a reliable source. Scripture can be that source for us. With God, Jesus and His teachings, and the Holy Spirit in us, we can find our way even through the toughest of our life's questions. The Lord will also provide for us someone here on earth to walk through the journey with us. I pray that you will open up to the possibilities of being vulnerable with who God leads you to.

A Journey is always more fun and productive if we are enjoying or taking our time through it. Even if it is hard, stick with it. Do not quit. If there is a detour or a bump on the path, we may have to stay there and work our way around it before we continue. That is okay. This is a process to finding our way to the end of this particular journey. Our life will have many journeys so we may have to work through the process many times.

Dig deep, be courageous, and trust in the One that desires for us to be with Him at the end of our journeys. Taking time and digging deep into our thoughts and feelings will bring more awareness and help with the healing process. Do not rush it! Pray to the Lord to help you find the answers you need and the healing you desire. Allowing the Lord to be a part of the process is key!

You will also find that asking someone to walk with you through this process will help keep you on the path of healing. This person can be a close friend or mentor who you have experience with and trust. This person should also be someone who will steer you in the direction of God and encourage you to grow in your relationship with Him. They should be willing to gently push you to get out of the imaginary box that you may have yourself in while loving you greatly through it all. They need not be, as Brene' Brown puts it, a "candle blower outer."

You could also hire a coach to collaborate with you. A coach is a trained person who will listen carefully and help draw out the best in you. A coach will ask you questions that will bring awareness to your mind that you may not be able to find on your own. A coach is a valuable resource since they will be on "your" side because they do not have an agenda, they are only there to see you get to where you want to go.

Here are tips to consider when working through your questions.

- **Mile Marker 1** is about discovering your question and why it is coming to the surface. Process through your question until you feel you are ready to move on.

- **Mile Marker 2** is about scripture and who you relate to in scripture. Knowing that someone else has had a similar experience or question and learning from them can help. God will lead you to them, so make sure you spend time getting to know them. This will bring a deeper awareness of who you are.

- **Mile Marker 3** is about searching through scripture to see what they say about your question or belief around your question. Not about the people but the subject.

- **Mile Marker 4** is about self-reflection. How do your beliefs around your questions show up in your daily walk and how does a new awareness move me to change?

- **Mile Marker 5** is about action. If there is no action, there is no movement which will lead to stagnation.

- **Mile Marker 6** is about routine. Doing a daily check-in helps you stay grounded.

- **Mile Marker "You are Here"** asks you to author your story. Be vulnerable and share life with someone who can learn from what God has taught you.

To be self-reflective, you will have to pull from feeling words that you may not have allowed yourself to use before. You may not even be able to come up with the right word. There are many feeling word lists available to use. Simply search the internet for "Feeling Word Lists" and you will find many. You may also find that seeking out the definition of a word will aid you in pinpointing your exact emotion. This is a journey remember, NOT A RACE!

TRUST THE PROCESS

Rhonda Gould

Coaching & Consulting

Flight Journey
Have you ever taken a trip that you needed to fly? I have! There have been several times when the plane had mechanical issues and I had to either change planes or wait on the tarmac. That change or delay did not stop me from getting to my destination. It simply adjusted the journey a bit.

The Crush

I find myself going back to the first time I remember being rejected. I know this may sound silly. What I am learning is that seemingly silly things can sometimes be the catapult that launches the internal value and thought processes. These values and thoughts can eventually, even years later, land you in a puddle. A puddle of heartache full of fear, shame, anger, and unworthiness.

As I told you before, I was nine and one-half when my baby sister was born. She was mine, or at least it felt like that. I would frequently put her in the stroller and roll her around our neighborhood, dressing her up and showing her off. She was a beauty, and I was proud to be her sister. At that age, boys are awkward, and girls are silly, but as far as crushes go, I had it bad for a little boy in our neighborhood. I was fascinated with him. It was a puppy love of sorts with hearts scribbled all over the page and thoughts of a fairytale ending. One day as I strolled my sister around, he came up to us. I was awe-struck and so excited that he had even given me the time of day. He asked if that was my baby sister and I replied, "yes, she is." I was beaming with pride at this point. I am thinking he is interested in me, until he said, "She is so pretty! It is too bad you are not as pretty as her." That crush on him crushed me! Even at 60, I can remember that day as if it were yesterday.

Now, remember, I said boys were awkward, and he may have even liked me. But that seemingly simple comment left rejection marks on me that have had lasting effects.

Rhonda's process through Mile Marker 1.

Verbalize our questions is the <u>1st step</u> to finding answers.

Our Father, who art in heaven, hallowed be thy name,

What is my question?

(my example) Why do others continue to reject me?

What has changed in my life and brought me to seek answers to this question?

(my example) In the last 3 years, I have lost 2 jobs, but the problem was not the loss of the job but the rejection that came with it.

What would it mean to me to find the answers to this question?

(my example) Healing of the inner critic that says: "I have no value;" "I am worthless;" "I'm expendable."

When we find ourselves asking questions, this usually means that we are finding ourselves questioning something that we have believed.

What belief is driving this question?

(my example) My sense of not being capable is holding me back from "going for it" with confidence and this lack of confidence is eating away at me. It is halting my motivation and starting to make me pull away from life and relationships.

What do I think God says about this belief?

(my example) I believe that God created me and has made me capable simply because I am His.

The next several pages are for you to start the work of processing your question.

I tell you, on the day of judgment people will give account for every careless word they speak. Matthew 12:36

 **"Ask Him": Use this space to spend some time with scripture. Read it multiple times and see what God reveals to you through it.**

Mark 11:24 Therefore I tell you, whatever you ask for in prayer, believe that you have received it, and it will be yours.

What is it telling me?

How does it change my perspective?

How is that perspective going to play out in my life?

For you, being able to verbalize your question is the <u>1st Step</u> to finding answers.

Our Father, who art in heaven, hallowed be thy name,

What is my question?

What has changed in my life and brought me to seek answers to this question?

What would it mean to me to find the answers to this question?

When we find ourselves asking questions, this usually means that we are finding ourselves questioning something that we have believed.

What belief is driving this question?

What do I think God says about this belief?

_____

_____

_____

_____

_____

_____

_____

_____

_____

_____

Love
Faithfulness
JOY
PATIENCE
Be the Fruit
Gal 5:22-23
peace
Self-control
Goodness
GENTLENESS
kindness

Gardening Journey
Easily distracted by flowers. I have that printed on a T-shirt. Flower gardening is a hobby for me, but I have learned that if I start by seed, I must be patient and water them so that they will germinate and grow. If I plant one that has already started the growing process, I still must nurture it so it will flourish. My journey is the same, I must be patient and nurture the process so I will grow through the process and arrive where I planned to be.

Unspoken Words

As I said in my last story, a simple comment can leave lasting effects. The thoughtless, unkind words of a little boy created thoughts in my head that said I needed to look a certain way to be worthy of love and attention. There are also times when nothing needs to be said for it to have lasting effects. The choices of someone else created beliefs that I had to be a certain way to be worthy and to have value. These beliefs led me down an unhealthy path that caused one rejection after another.

When emotional or physical violations occur against someone so young, it is often very confusing. As a child, I did not understand those violations would shape my mind causing me to believe those heinous actions were somehow good and appropriate. When I became an adult, I just thought that being taken advantage of or being abused was normal. Believing that was how I would be shown love. And if I did not agree with how I was being treated, then I would be pushed aside, rejected. I believed that allowing someone else to use me as they pleased was the only way to receive love from them. I did not even allow myself to feel. There were times when I believed it was what I wanted or deserved

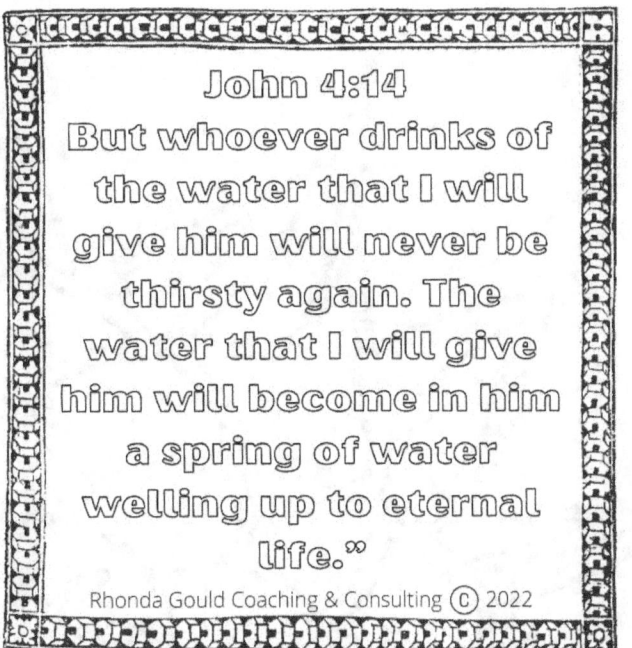

John 4:14
But whoever drinks of the water that I will give him will never be thirsty again. The water that I will give him will become in him a spring of water welling up to eternal life."

Rhonda Gould Coaching & Consulting © 2022

Later as an adult, I remember having a conversation with my son about the young girls he was around. And according to what he said to me, those young girls too, believed that is what they wanted, most likely because of the same belief system. I have since learned that it is just part of the effects of trauma. Unfortunately, our minds at that age, are not mature enough to understand any different.

Now please understand, that I did not have Jesus in my life at the time. But even if I had, it may not have spared me. I may as well have been, Mary Magdalene or the woman at the well. My choices, because of those thoughts and beliefs, held me captive in negative behaviors. I experienced rejection because I was either very promiscuous or not promiscuous enough. And with every rejection came the shame, guilt, and confusion that left more lasting marks on my heart and soul. Those marks were quickly becoming scars.

Rhonda's process through Mile Marker 2.

Knowing that you are not alone in your beliefs or questions is the **2nd Step** to finding answers and healing.

thy kingdom come, thy will be done, on earth as it is in heaven.

Who is in the Bible that may have had a similar belief or situation?

(my example) Mary Magdalene : Matthew 27:56, 61; 28:1; Mark 15:40, 47, 16:1, 9; Luke 8:2, 24:10; and John 19:25, 20:1, 11, 18.

- *Why do I relate to him/her? She was a prostitute and due to the nature of the very beginning of my violation, my value was led in a direction that caused me to have more rejection.*

- *Where was he/she from? Magdala, is a town on the western shore of the Sea of Galilee.*

- *What was him/her nature? Loyal and generous*

Woman at the Well: John 4:4-42

Why do I relate to him/her?

Because of her past (I am sure), she made mistakes that lead her to make bad decisions and caused the town to reject her. Not only was she rejected by her people, but she grew up in life and culture where she was rejected by the neighboring Jews.

- Where was he/she from? *Samaria*
- What was his/her nature? *Withdrawn, believer, and faithful*

What do the scriptures say about this belief? *(my belief is "I am not capable")*

(my example) I am not capable on my own. It is Jesus that makes me capable, valued, worthy & loved. It is He, that makes me whole. It is He, that I need to serve, not man.

Scripture reference:

1 John 3:1 - See what kind of love the Father has given to us, that we should be called children of God; and so, we are. The reason why the world does not know us is that it did not know him.

Scripture reference:

Galatians 2:20- I have been crucified with Christ. It is no longer I who live, but Christ who lives in me. And the life I now live in the flesh I live by faith in the Son of God, who loved me and gave himself for me.

Scripture reference:

Romans 8:37 - No, in all these things we are more than conquerors through him who loved us.

Scripture reference:

Ephesians 3:17-19 - So that Christ may dwell in your hearts through faith—that you, being rooted and grounded in love, may have the strength to comprehend with all the saints what is the breadth and length and height and depth, and to know the love of Christ that surpasses knowledge, that you may be filled with all the fullness of God.

Now that I know what scripture says about this belief, is my belief a truth or is it a lie?

(my example) Lie

Satan is the creator of lies. He knows me well, regretfully, and he will use anything, even the small stuff, to create in me fear, shame, or guilt. He will twist the truth so that it can seem like a lie and take a lie to make it seem true. My truth should only come from scripture.

The next several pages are for you to start the work of processing your question.

 **"Need Him": Use this space to spend some time with scripture. Read it multiple times and see what God reveals to you through it.**

Philippians 4:19 And my God will meet all your needs according to the riches of his glory in Christ Jesus.

What is it telling me?

How does it change my perspective?

How is that perspective going to play out in my life?

For you, knowing that you are not alone in your beliefs or questions is the 2nd Step to finding answers and healing.

thy kingdom come, thy will be done, on earth as it is in heaven.

Who is in the Bible that may have had a similar belief or situation?

- *Why do I relate to him/her?*

- *Where was he/she from?*

- *What was his/her nature?*

What do the scriptures say about this belief?

Scripture reference:

_____

_____

Scripture reference:

_____

_____

Scripture reference:

_____

_____

Now that I know what scripture says about this belief, is my belief a truth or is it a lie?

_____

_____

_____

_____

_____

_____

_____

_____

_____

_____

_____

_____

_____

Progress not Perfection

Rhonda Gould Coaching & Consulting

Motorcycle Journey

I love riding my motorcycle. Out on the open road with all of God's creation and the smells that go along with it. I was having a problem with my gas gauge not reading correctly so I never knew how much gas I had left. This did not stop me though. I would keep up with the miles and when I had traveled around 100 miles, I would just stop and fill up. This did not stop me from doing what I loved, it simply caused me to be more aware during the journey.

The Perfect Life

As I spoke of in "The Crush" story, the rejection through simple words took hold of me and was the first of my rejection marks. These rejection marks were now becoming scars as I moved into my marriage with my first husband. I know that we all bring scars or "baggage" into our marriages, but I brought more than just a carry-on. Everything was changing when I met him. As a senior in high school, I was attending church and was baptized. I had no clue what I was doing at all. I was not raised in the church, nor was there even the mention of God. I did not think I fit the mold of a real Christian. I believed that I needed to change everything about myself and the way I lived. I was partially correct. What I did not know was that it was not me who was going to be doing the "needed" change. It was Jesus in my life, through the Holy Spirit that would start the change and carry it through.

My first husband had everything I did not have. He was raised in a Christian home; I was not. His family was always nearby; mine was not. They went to church together, spent Sunday afternoons together, prepared meals, and played. This is what I was looking for; this is what I believed God had handed me. I believed that God had given me the perfect man, the perfect family, the perfect church, which would lead to the perfect life. Boy was I wrong! I did not realize that just because you did all the "right things," like going to church regularly, did not make you perfect. I was only a few weeks into our marriage when I realized that perfection was not what I got, and perfection was not what I could give.

A year into the marriage was the first explosive realization, as I was glancing over a phone bill and noticed multiple conversations with a mutual female friend during a time I was out of town. The rejection knife cut yet again. When I confronted the reasons for these calls, I found out that her marriage was struggling, and my husband was filling in the spaces that she needed, and he wanted. I also worked with this woman which made the blow even stronger. This was only the beginning of explosive realizations and rejections. Then ten years and multiple affairs/rejection marks later, I found myself divorced with two small children. Marks that were brought on by the choices of another not only cut me but now they were affecting two other little people. A new kind of heartache was added to the pain in my soul and the scars were getting deeper every time.

Rhonda's process through Mile Marker 3.

Seeking out and living in the truth is the <u>3rd Step</u> to finding answers and healing.

Give us this day our daily bread.

What do I believe scripture says about my specific question or subject?

(my example) I believe that it says, man may reject me, but God will never reject me. I need to find a way to not listen to man and fix my thoughts on God's word.

Scripture reference:

Romans 8:31 - What then shall we say to these things? If God is for us, who can be against us?

Scripture reference:

Isaiah 43:4-5 - Because you are precious in my eyes and honored, and I love you, I give men in return for you, peoples in exchange for your life. Fear not, for I am with you; I will bring your offspring from the east, and from the west I will gather you.

Scripture reference:

1 Peter 1:17-21 Since you call on a Father who judges each person's work impartially, live out your time as foreigners here in reverent fear. For you know that it was not with perishable things such as silver or gold that you were redeemed from the empty way of life handed down to you from your ancestors, but with the precious blood of Christ, a lamb without blemish or defect. He was chosen before the creation of the world but was revealed in these last times for your sake. Through him, you believe in God, who raised him from the dead and glorified him, and so your faith and hope are in God.

What do these scriptures tell me about this question or subject?

(my example) My hope is in God. He will never reject me, and he will never leave me to wander alone. God brought me to Jesus and the Holy Spirit to guide me in my walk. I will trust Him.

The next several pages are for you to start the work of processing your question.

 **"Seek Him": Use this space to spend some time with scripture. Read it multiple times and see what God reveals to you through it.**

Hebrews 11:6 And without faith it is impossible to please God because anyone who comes to him must believe that he exists and that he rewards those who earnestly seek him.

What is it telling me?

How does it change my perspective?

How is that perspective going to play out in my life?

For you, seeking out and living in the truth is the 3rd Step to finding answers and healing.

Give us this day our daily bread.

What do I believe scripture says about my specific question or subject?

Scripture reference:

_____

_____

Scripture reference:

_____

_____

Scripture reference:

_____

_____

Scripture reference:

_____

_____

What do these scriptures tell me about this question or subject?

_____

_____

_____

_____

_____

_____

_____

_____

_____

_____

_____

_____

_____

_____

_____

_____

_____

_____

If you *Return* to ME I will RESTORE *You*

Jeremiah 15:19

Rhonda Gould

Coaching & Consulting

Journey with Road Construction

On motorcycles, we usually travel the back roads so when there is road construction it can delay our journey. On this particular trip, we had to take a detour that delayed our arrival by several hours and through some remote back roads. But the sights we saw through that detour were fantastic. We embraced the beauty that we received through it. Our destination was not changed, the journey was simply enhanced.

Friendship

Friendships as children are typically easy and carefree. You meet each other, and you play together. It is simple, happy, and joyous! That is what I remember.

Friendships as adults are a bit trickier. Every person grows into someone that has thought patterns and behaviors that have been molded because of their pasts. How they were raised, what their parents modeled for them, and if they experienced trauma, form who they are.

This is the story of a friendship rejected. My family had blended with another family so perfectly. We had lots of laughs and good times. Many hours were spent playing together with our children playing and going to church. As time passes, children age and decisions get harder.

One day I found myself unexpectantly sitting across the table from a very dear friend and her husband. "They" had decided that confronting me about a situation and my decision-making about our son was needed. I had no problem being confronted because that is an important part of close friendship. The confrontation was not the issue. It was that the confrontation was not presented in love or with any sense of grace. It was presented in a way that I was attacked for not being the perfect parent. My friend's husband believed he was perfect in this area, and I needed to get it right. I sat there almost paralyzed in total

Proverbs 15:1
A soft answer turns away wrath, but a harsh word stirs up anger.

Rhonda Gould Coaching & Consulting © 2022

disbelief that my dear friend was not defending me against this attack. Her husband was spewing venom at me, but she just sat there. When he finally finished, I was in shock, a fragile shell that had been broken to pieces. I could not talk, cry, or even move. I was fractured, and our friendship was fractured. These were friends I trusted and believed loved me, so the rejection marks ran deep.

Rhonda's process through Mile Marker 4.

Recognizing the answers that God has given you through scripture is the **4th Step** to finding answers and healing.

And forgive us our debts, as we forgive our debtors

What answers have I found so far?

(my example) I have realized that I put too much weight into what others think, and I do not depend on God enough.

How does my trust in scripture show up in my day-to-day, concerning this question or subject?

(my example) I am learning not to internalize the feelings of others. They are for them to feel, not me. I am also turning more to scripture for my internal feelings.

How does my trust in this belief show up in my day-to-day?

(my example) I have the urge to talk to anyone who will listen to me, for my own, personal conformation, instead of talking to God and feeling His presence.

What thoughts may I need to change, so I can trust and live within God's truth more?

(my example) Unvalued – God says I am His - Matthew 6:26

(my example) Not Worthy – God says He made me worthy - Phil 1:6

What answers have I gotten from what I have learned about my belief and God's word?

(my example) That God made me, and he does not make mistakes. He has a greater plan for me and will make me capable to carry out that plan. And when I waiver from His plan, He will stick by me through the tough times until I get back on track.

What needs to change in my answer-finding process, the next time I have a question?

(my example) I need to go to Him in prayer first. Then I need to go to scripture. I also need to let some time pass and <u>wait</u> for Him to bring awareness to my soul. Reach out to the people I know who are safe: those that God placed in my life.

What other references could I use to help me find answers?

(my example) Concordances, Bible dictionaries, and websites on the topic to find out more information. as well as friends who have had the same experiences. The Lord will provide you with discernment if you pray for it.

Although our relationship with God, Jesus, and the Holy Spirit should always be the first step in finding answers, seeking truth, finding healing, and moving on, having people in our lives who care about our walk with Christ is vital to our healing from our beliefs and questions. People will do this by encouraging us to seek out God's truths/answers and holding us accountable for walking with Him. Again, pray to God for discernment when it comes to opening up to the right people.

Who is my support group to help me stay on the path of finding TRUTH answers?

(my example) Thankfully, I have several women that I can go for support and encouragement. I must admit that early on in my journey, I knew who I could go to for truth or who I could go to so I could hear what I wanted to hear. The friends (you know who you are) that say the truth in love are the keepers.

The next several pages are for you to start the work of processing your question.

**"Woo You": Use this space to spend some time with scripture. Read it multiple times and see what God reveals to you through it.**

Job 36:16 "He is wooing you from the jaws of distress to a spacious place free from restriction, to the comfort of your table laden with choice food.

What is it telling me?

How does it change my perspective?

How is that perspective going to play out in my life?

For you, recognizing the answers that God has given you through scripture is the <u>4th Step</u> to finding answers and healing.

And forgive us our debts, as we forgive our debtors

What answers have I found so far?

How does my trust in scripture show up in my day-to-day, concerning this question or subject?

How does my trust in the belief show up in my day-to-day?

What thoughts may I need to change, so I can trust and live within God's truth more?

What answers have I gotten from what I have learned about my belief and God's word?

What needs to change in my answer-finding process the next time I have a question?

What other references could I use to help me find answers?

Although our relationship with God, Jesus, and the Holy Spirit should always be the first step in finding answers, seeking truth, finding healing, and moving on. Having people in our lives who care about our walk with Christ is vital to our healing from our beliefs and questions. People will do this by encouraging us to seek out God's truths/answers and holding us accountable for walking with Him. Again, pray to God for discernment when it comes to opening up to the right people.

Who is my support group to help me stay on the path of finding TRUTH answers?

_____

_____

_____

_____

_____

_____

Let go of what you can't Control

Proverbs 3:5-6

Fishing Journey
My husband and I took our boat out on the water to do some fishing on a lake with which we were not familiar. We were so enjoying the fishing, in and out of little coves and drifting in the shade of the trees as the breeze moved the boat on the water. Hours passed when we realized we had gotten lost in the journey. After gathering our thoughts, we simply had to ask for help on our journey that day.

God's Calling

My husband and I had moved to Kentucky, just after my 50th birthday! That was a big one! But in some ways, it felt like I was being reborn. Before the move, I had lived in the same area and went to the same church for 25 years. Even though I was an adult when I moved there, I felt like I had grown up in that church. I walked into that church as a newly married woman with one small son. This church family walked with me through the addition of another son, a struggling marriage, and a divorce. They celebrated with me in a new marriage and helped me carry the burden of a son with cancer and a rebelling son. They were my family. I was involved with the youth program there and active in the women's programs. There was a lot of rejoicing, and there was a lot of pain during those 25 years. But after it was all said and done, I realized I was still standing and ready for God's new adventure.

"When you pass through the waters, I will be with you; and when you pass through the rivers, they will not sweep over you. When you walk through the fire, you will not be burned; the flames will not set you ablaze."
Isaiah 43:2
Rhonda Gould Coaching & Consulting © 2022

Not only had I weathered pain, but I had walked with many women while they weathered their pains. Together we had played, studied God's word, cried, and learned. So, as challenging as it was to leave and start from scratch, I felt like it was time to go. I know God was calling me to minister to the women in Kentucky. So, I walked out of that church stronger and better equipped to serve the Lord.

A little bit of what I have learned over the last several years is this: if you believe you feel God's nudging then you might need to have some conversations with Him and let Him guide your steps before simply forging your way through the fields. I felt called. I believed that He had qualified me. I had listened to the needs of the women. So, full steam ahead I went, not considering this small town did not know me at all. This Kentucky church was steeped in its traditions, and just because I heard God calling, it did not mean they had heard it too.

The full steam ahead led me to the desire to start a woman's ministry. Because of history that I was not aware of and people who were already in place at one of our satellite campuses, it was decided that she would lead the ministry. I was okay with this plan because my only desire was that the women of my church have a place to grow in their spiritual walk and grow in their ability to see who God created them to be. Plans were made, people became interested, and the process began to have a woman's ministry. But through this transition, a conversation I had with one of the women involved in my new church went like this, "If you were trying to make a name for yourself. You did! But not in the way you may have wanted to". "Ouch, that hurt.", I can remember thinking to myself. I understand that she did not know me at all, but my heart broke yet again. Because of the scars that had already begun forming, even the smallest of cuts dig deep.

Rhonda's process through the Mile Marker 5.

Putting your understanding of God's truth into action in your life is the 5<u>th</u> Step to finding answers and healing.

And lead us not into temptation; but deliver us from evil.

What is my action plan that will lead me to live a day of healing from my beliefs and finding answers? *(my example)*

1. I will be in the word daily, even if it is just for a few scriptures and prayer.

2. I will ask God to help me fight against Satan's attack on my mind.

3. I will turn to friends who I know to love me with the love of God for support & encouragement.

Who are "my people" that will help me stay on track with healing?

Identify 2-3 people that you will be able to reach out to. It is vital to have more than one so that we do not overload our friends who are dealing with their own burdens. See Ecclesiastes 4:12, "Though one may be overpowered, two can defend themselves. A cord of three strands is not quickly broken." Remember, you too can be that person for them.

1. (I have several in mind)

2.

3.

1 John 4:19
We love because he first
loved us.

The next several pages are for you to start the work of

processing your question.

"Encourage You": Use this space to spend some time with scripture. Read it multiple times and see what God reveals to you.

Jeremiah 29:11 For I know the plans I have for you," declares the LORD, "plans to prosper you and not to harm you, plans to give you hope and a future.

What is it telling me?

How does it change my perspective?

How is that perspective going to play out in my life?

For you, putting your understanding of God's truth into action in your life is the 5th Step to finding answers and healing.

And lead us not into temptation; but deliver us from evil.

What is my action plan that will lead me to live a day of healing from my beliefs and finding answers?

1.

2.

3.

Who are "my people" that will help me stay on track with healing?

Identify 2-3 people that you will be able to reach out to. It is vital to have more than one so that we do not overload our friends who are dealing with their own burdens. See Ecclesiastes 4:12, "Though one may be overpowered, two can defend themselves. A cord of three strands is not quickly broken."

1.

2.

3.

Above you chose 3 friends who are "your people". What attributes contribute to them being on this list? What experiences have you walked with them through? How have you changed because of their presence in your life? How are you living out those attributes yourself?

_____

_____

_____

_____

_____

_____

_____

_____

_____

_____

_____

_____

_____

_____

_____

_____

_____

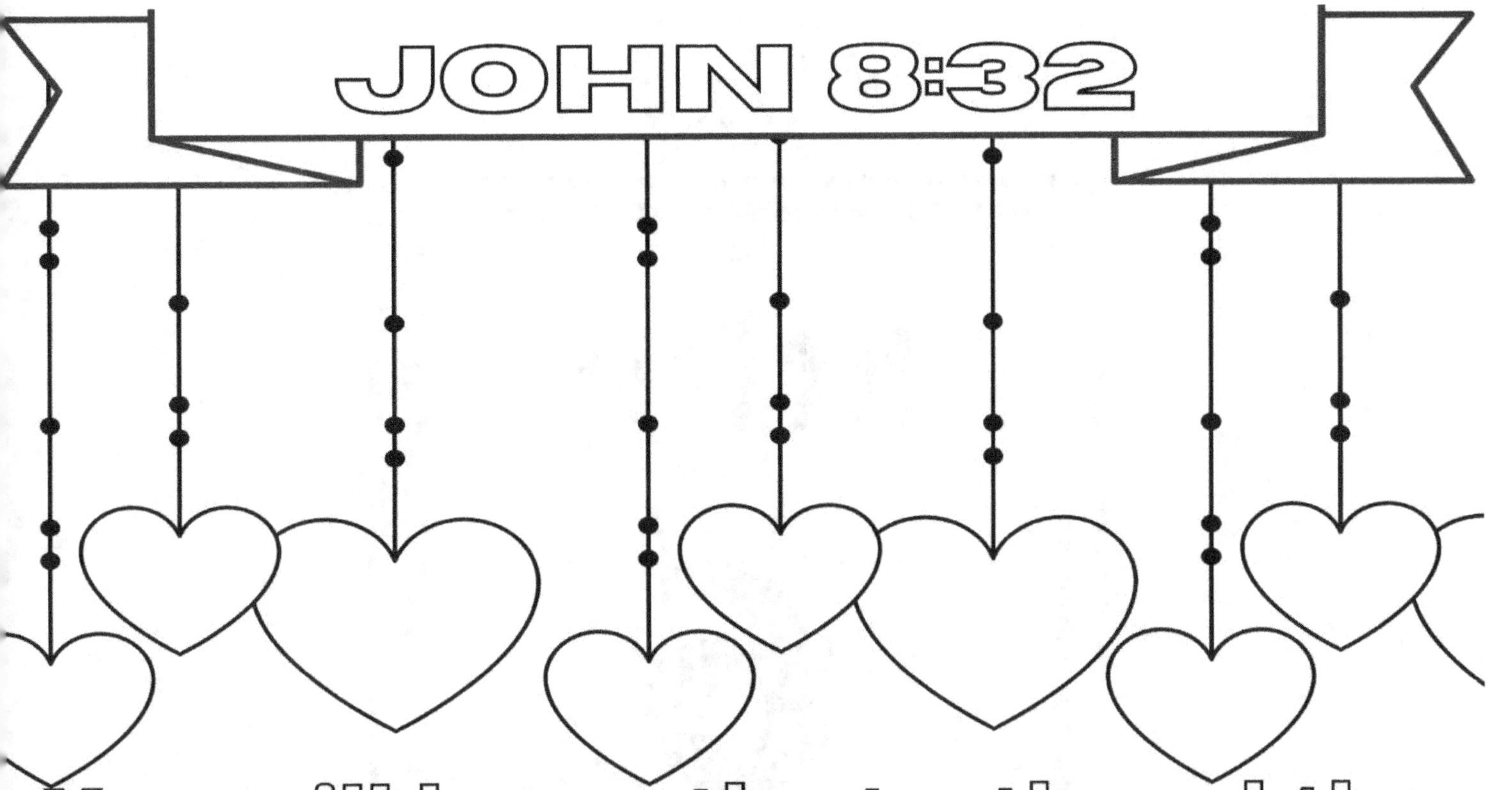

JOHN 8:32

You will know the truth and the truth will set you free

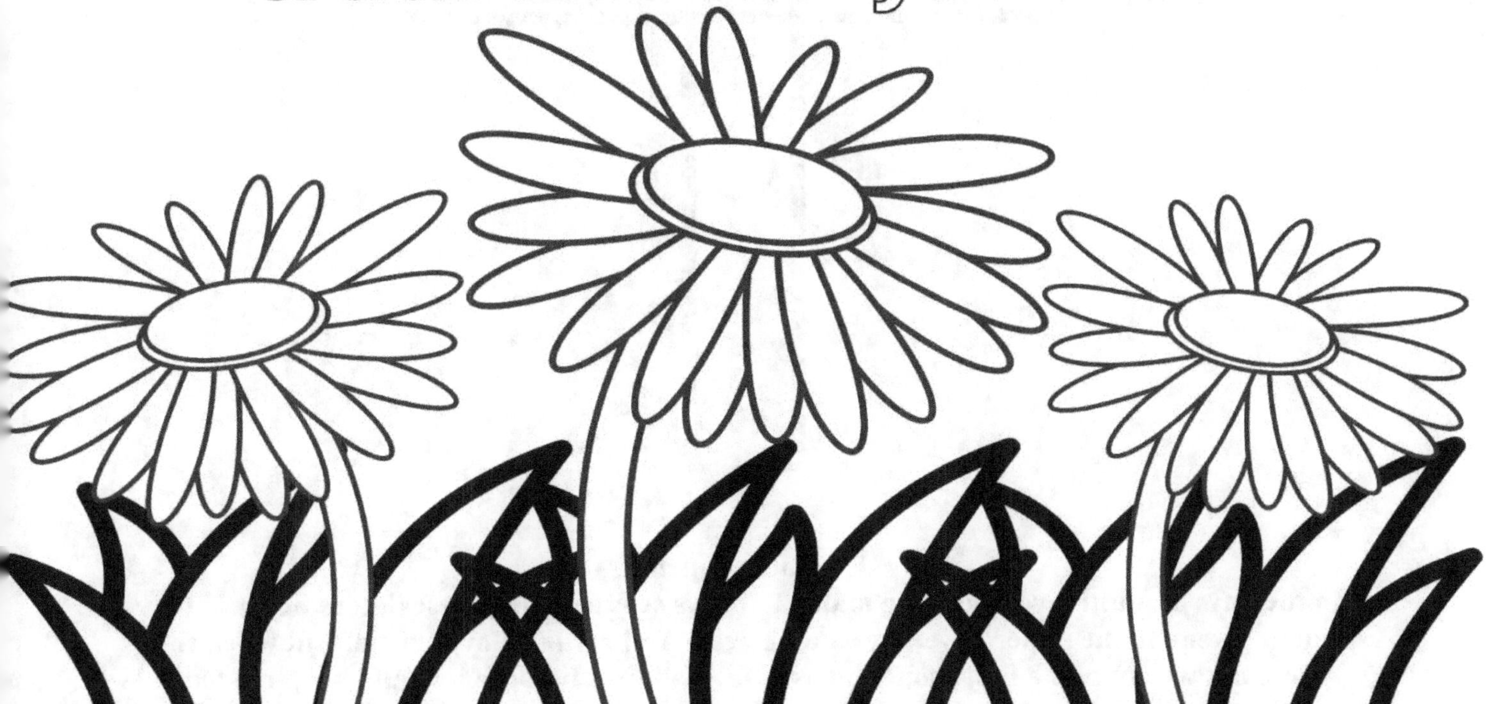

Mile

6

Escalator Journey
In the days of multi-level shopping malls, I always scouted out the escalators because they would get me to the upper/lower levels with ease. And my kids loved them. But when they were not working, the first thought was "Oh, No". Not because it would keep me from getting to the next level but because it would take a bit more effort from me to get there. That is how my journeys have been.

Out of the Closet

Many years have passed by this point. I have remarried. My children have grown up and have children of their own. On the outside, I have it together. On the inside, the pieces of me that had been catapulted into the air were starting to fall to the ground. All the many rejected pieces that had come from years of crushing shame, guilt, confusion, and heartache were falling and I could not catch them and make them stop. Yet I knew there was more to come. This was the time for all my pieces to fall.

I joined a group at church called Celebrate Recovery and started the process to become a leader. Remember, on the outside, I had it all together. This is where the pieces began to fall. While going through the 12-step process, I finally came out of the darkness. Shedding light on the abuse that I had endured as a child was the first step to breaking free, and for the first time in years, I felt a weight lifted. Of course, God was not finished with His Refiner's Fire just yet. His loving nudge said, "There are more pieces that must fall." The pieces that would confront the sexual abuse both emotionally and physically. The weight of the denial was lifted from me, but the weight of abuse and damages caused were now going to be placed on the innocent. There was no way around it and that was not part of my plan.

I fought Him for a while until I could not fight any longer. Now it was time to bring others into the pile of broken pieces.

Over the next several years, the fight against good and evil became very real in my life. There were tears and fears running rampant in my body. But I heard Him say, "It is time to open the door wide. I will be with you." He reminded me of what Jeremiah 29:11-13 says: "'For I know the plans I have for you,' declares the LORD, 'plans to prosper you and not to harm you, plans to give you hope and a future. Then you will call on me and come and pray to me, and I will listen to you. You will seek me and find me when you seek me with all your heart.'"

On the day that He walked with me to push the door open all the way to let every ounce of His light shine was also when the doors closed to other relationships. The denial that God had lifted off of me was now weighing heavy on the shoulder of the abuser. I knew I was fully free, but this freedom came with a very high price. Satan once again tried to use the wounds of rejection to crush my heart one more time.

Rhonda Gould Coaching & Consulting © 2022

Rhonda's process through the Mile Marker 6.

For you, daily self-reflection along with seeking scripture regularly is necessary.

This is the 6th <u>Step</u>.

For thine is the kingdom, and the power, and the glory, for ever and ever. Amen.

Step 6 is about my **Daily Check-in** with God. Making sure that I keep that line open to Him and asking Him to join me. Letting Him know my fears, my joys, my pain, my dreams, and my desire to know Him more fully. Giving Him thanks for everything that I have seen and continue to see Him doing in my life. I am still living a life here on earth with the inherent sin all around me, and I am repeatedly reminded of that fact. That reminder also acts as a notice that I still needed Him. So daily, I walk through this guide. I may not do it all at one time. I may only discuss bits and pieces of it with Him, and He is patient with me. He longs for my voice to call out to Him, and He listens.

How do you feel today and why? (Find a word that describes how you feel.) *(my example)*

Today I believe… *I am loved and enough because I am HIS.*

I believe this **<u>because</u>**… *History is the true storyteller and Scripture tells me it is so.*

I have believed this **<u>before</u>** when… *At 60, I am just starting to live this belief because of leaning into scripture and a relationship with HIM more.*

I started to think *I had no worth or value before I understood & believed I am loved & enough because Jesus Christ died for me, so I go straight to prayer and scripture*

My **prayer** today is…

Lord, keep your words in my heart and mind as I walk through my days.

The next several pages are for you to start the work of processing your question.

 **"Reveal to You": Use this space to spend some time with scripture. Read it multiple times and see what God reveals to you through it.**

Revelation 3:20 Here I am! I stand at the door and knock. If anyone hears my voice and opens the door, I will come in and eat with that person, and they with me.

What is it telling me?

How does it change my perspective?

How is that perspective going to play out in my life?

For you, daily self-reflection along with seeking scripture regularly is necessary. This is the 6th Step.

For thine is the kingdom, and the power, and the glory, and ever. Amen.

Daily Check-in

How do you feel today and why? (Find one word that describes how you feel.)

Today I believe…

I believe this **because**…

I have believed this **before** when…

I start to think _____ when
I believe this way.

What do I do when I believe this way?

What does scripture say about this belief?

What does scripture say about me?

Because scripture is God's truth, today I choose to believe

Talk with God. Tell Him what you need, want, desire, and hope for. Do not hold back! He is listening to you! My **prayer** today is…

_____

_____

_____

_____

_____

_____

Jeremiah 29:11 For I know the plans I have for you," declares the Lord, "plans to prosper you and not to harm you, plans to give you hope and a future.

Heaven Journey
John 14:6 Jesus said to him, "I am the way, and the truth, and the life. No one comes to the Father except through me." My journeys have taken many wrong turns, but He continued to get me on the right path. I sometimes still take the path full of potholes and His great mercy continues to find me. Because of my relationship with Jesus and the knowledge that one day I will be with God in Heaven, my journey is easier than it would be without Him.

Redemptive Story

I am sitting here at my desk, the keyboard at my fingertips and I do not know where to start. My redemptive story is amazing. Do not get me wrong. My life is not all roses and rainbows or lollipops and cakes, but it is a story that only the Lord could have written.

So, where do I begin? The last 10 years, here in Kentucky, have been a blur, yet they have been the clearest I have ever had. Understanding that He was walking with me through every painful step, holding me up, wiping my tears, and carrying me when needed. There is no doubt that if I had been without Him, I would not be where I am: standing in this home, with my husband, my children, and my biggest blessings, my grandchildren. I am loving every minute of this life, even the still painful ones, because I know He will come through for me again and again, and again.

Yes, I have lost some relationships in the process, but I still pray for those relationships. I pray that the Lord will work in them and restore them before time runs out. I pray for their souls to be renewed with the rejoicing of who God is to them. I pray that their hearts will be softened, and their minds will become clear. I pray for me to be in a steady relationship with HIM.

Yes, I have restored my relationship with my friend who I mentioned in my "Friendship" story, which was once fractured. Imagine the pain of the rejection I felt but God gave me the strength and the courage to sit down with her and be honest and vulnerable. Through that conversation, we cried, and she was open about the pain she felt through the experience. Thankfully, God was in her heart and gave her the spirit to hear me. Yes, it was hard. But Jesus was standing there and joined in the conversation, so the restoration could be seen and felt. As painful as that experience was, I am grateful that God allowed us to enter that journey together.

Through this experience, we found what a true, Jesus-loving, forgiving, grace-filled, and mercy-flowing friendship is. He showed Himself fully in it.

Yes, the loss of particularly important relationships feels heavy and weighs on my soul, and at times I feel paralyzed by the grief, yet Jesus lifts the weight so I can breathe. He was and is still at work in those relationships, I am sure. But until it is time for restoration, He shows His mercy for me in big, fantastic, and unexpected ways. Just as He did by bringing my birthfather back into my life, after being apart for 50 years. I would tell my dad, "It was all in God's perfect timing." Acts 1:7 says, "He said to them, 'It is not for you to know times or seasons that the Father has fixed by his own authority'".

Just as God's timing is perfect in the circumstances around me. His timing that is working within my soul is made perfect so that I can accept His perfect grace and mercy that is given so freely. I must wait in His timing with peace that surpasses all understanding.

This is only a glimpse into my redemptive story. God has done so much more! And I am full only because I believe what it says in Philippians 3:12-14, "Not that I have already obtained this or am already perfect, but I press on to make it my own because Christ Jesus has made me his own. Brothers, I do not consider that I have made it my own. But one thing I do: forgetting what lies behind and straining forward to what lies ahead, I press on toward the goal for the prize of the upward call of God in Christ Jesus."

This verse helps me understand that I must never stand still, I must always keep moving. I can choose to move forward or choose to move backward. I choose forward!

Please pray with me.

God grant me the serenity to accept the things I cannot change, the courage to change the things I can, and the wisdom to know the difference. Living one day at a time, enjoying one moment at a time, accepting hardships as the pathway to peace, taking, as He did, this sinful world as it is, not as I would have it, trusting that He will make things right if I surrender to His Will, so that I may be reasonably happy in this life, and supremely happy with Him Forever and ever in the next. Amen.

Zephaniah 3:17
The Lord your God is in your midst, a mighty one who will save; he will rejoice over you with gladness; he will quiet you by his love; he will exult over you with loud singing.

Rhonda Gould Coaching & Consulting © 2022

God grant me the serenity to accept the things I cannot change; Courage to change the things I can;

Rhonda's process through He Saves.

He Saves section is when you look in Scripture for where Jesus was rejected or teaching about rejection.

Scripture reference:

Jesus tells the parable of the tenants in Matt 21, Mark 12, and Luke 20 to give his listeners an understanding of what is to come. It was commonplace for landowners to rent out the land and then come to collect their share. In this story, the "tenants" were not wanting to give up their share of the profits. They chose to do evil and harm, so they would inherit the land. This parable shows how God has sent others to teach his people, and they have chosen to not listen and do as they will. Then He sends his son, Jesus, believing they will respect and honor Him, but they do not.

I wonder how am I rejecting Jesus with my actions? Am I killing everyone around me so that I can be the winner in this game of life? Am I refusing to submit to God's will, Jesus, with my disobedience and need for power and wealth? Am I more concerned about how others perceive me rather than how God perceives me?

What might I need to be learning?

I need to trust Him more fully and recognize when it is Him speaking to me or Satan speaking to me.

Scripture reference:

Proverbs 15:31-33, Whoever heeds life-giving correction will be at home among the wise. Those who disregard discipline despise themselves, but the one who heeds correction gains understanding. Wisdom's instruction is to fear the LORD, and humility comes before honor.

Lord, I come to you today humbled by what you have shown me. Let my ears hear you and let my heart soak in your teaching. Help me to release my need to control and overcome with power by me submitting my will to You. Help me to look to You for my inheritance of heaven and be willing to do what is good and right in Your eyes, not in man's. I love and praise Your Holy Name. Amen

The next several pages are for you to start the work of processing your question.

He will "Save You": Use this space to spend some time with scripture.

Read it multiple times and see what God reveals to you through it.

John 3:16 For God so loved the world that he gave his one and only Son, that whoever believes in him shall not perish but have eternal life.

Romans 6:23 For the wages of sin is death, but the gift of God is eternal life in Christ Jesus our Lord.

What is it telling me?

How does it change my perspective?

How is that perspective going to play out in my life?

Author your own redemptive story. You may have several redemptive stories, so feel free to break them down into many small ones.

Author's Thoughts for You

If you are walking through this life, in the closet of darkness, my heart aches for you. If you feel alone, ashamed, guilt-ridden, if you cannot sleep or always sleep, if your mind never shuts off and you must stay constantly busy, or if you are not motivated to move, I have been where you are. When you wake, what are your first thoughts? Our minds can be our worst enemies. Even when everything appears to be good on the outside, our inside can still be in turmoil. What healthy ways do you refocus your mind? Please remember, if you are on prescribed medications or have physical limitations because of an illness always consult your physician before making any drastic changes.

It is said that physical activity is one of the best mind healers because when our body is tired our minds start shutting down also. Have you ever noticed that? Physical activity will help you feel less tense and even more motivated to move. It also plays a vital role in how your body feels by releasing your muscles and relaxing you to the point where your body can rest and even wants to rest. I do this by flower gardening.

Diet plays a part in our minds as well. You may have to play around with this and see what works for you. Keep a diary or journal of your food intake and how you are feeling. You also need to note the time of day that you are eating certain foods. See if you can connect the dots between what you eat and how you feel either physically or emotionally. For me, refined sugars have a dramatic effect on my body and mind. What are you willing to do to heal your mind and body?

Your environment can also take its toll on your mind. Work can be a big culprit in mind games. Ask yourself these questions. How am I fulfilled by the work I do, or how am I working on the purpose that God has set out for me? How do I feel valued or appreciated? How is the mental well-being of those around me? This is important because our minds are easily influenced by the words we hear. Is my workspace safe? What is something that needs to change about my work environment? How might a radio help? Making sure your work environment is good for your mental state will improve your whole mind and body. According to Gettysburg College research at https://www.gettysburg.edu/news/stories?id=79db7b34-630c-4f49-ad32-4ab9ea48e72b, One-third of a person's life span is spent at work. How is your work environment affecting your mind?

And now we move from work to home. Whether you work outside the home or work inside the home, the other two-thirds of your life is where you live. What is that environment like? Are you safe? Please, if you do not feel safe, reach out to someone that can and wants to help you. In what ways is your home peaceful? Are your needs being met? Having our needs met, whether physical, emotional, or spiritual, will play a role in how we feel. And do not get confused, I am talking about needs, not wants. What things need to change, if any, in your home environment?

Some other questions to consider are, how are you spending your free time and who are you spending it with? People are important to us. God created us for relationships, and if we are not cultivating good, solid, spirit-filled relationships, then our minds and bodies will wither. From the beginning of time, God said in Genesis, "It is not good for man to be alone." If relationships were not important, then God would not have emphasized "love" so much in His teachings. How is your love bank being filled by those around you? How are you loving yourself? Where are you going to find the right people to fill your life? It is okay to recognize those who take more than they give and therefore drain you. It is okay to walk away from those relationships. But pray first and seek God's guidance. Relationships are precious to the Lord, and He wants you to experience that here on earth. I heard a word the other day that spoke to me about my life and relationships. It was "Laughtatherapy." How much laughter do you have in your life? How are those in your world filling or taking away from you?

Most importantly, what spaces in your life are you allowing God's love to penetrate your mind and body? If you do not know the Lord your God, please find a church full of people who want nothing more than to fill you with the love that Christ came and died for. If you are already attending a church, how are you serving in a way that glorifies God, and how are you allowing others to serve you? He will fill you and supply all your needs. Reach out to HIM.

- Do not withdraw

- Do not ignore your feelings

- Be okay with your choices

- Be willing to fail and get back up

Lord, I come to you with a humble and still heart thanking you for all that you have done for me, thanking you for bringing me to a place of peace, and allowing me to understand that comfort does not always equal peace. That it is in the uncomfortable spaces that you let me sit that I will find my peace. Lord, I ask you into the lives of the readers of this prayer. Help them to lean into your love. Help them to carve out space for you until their whole being is filled. Speak to them in a way that they will hear you until You are the only One, they are listening to.

Lord, continue to wrap your arms around us and help us feel the safety within them.

Amen.

Don't look back

you are not going
that way !

Rhonda Gould Coaching & Consulting

The following pages are the process straight through. I pray that this process helps you find healing by answering the questions that linger in your thoughts. Finding answers allows your mind to rest. Answering the questions will make your heart more peaceful and seeking out God's word will draw you to a closer and more intimate relationship with Him.

He is with you always.

He will never leave you.

He created you in His image, and you are worthy.

He will guide your steps.

He will settle your soul.

He will give you wisdom and discernment.

He will make all things possible.

He has a great plan for you.

He loves you more than you could imagine.

He is your hope.

He is your peace.

He is your reason.

 **For you, being able to verbalize your question is the <u>1st Step</u> to finding answers.**

Our Father, who art in heaven, hallowed be thy name,

What is my question?

What has changed in my life and brought me to seek answers to this question?

What would it mean to me to find the answers to this question?

When we find ourselves asking questions, this usually means that we are finding ourselves questioning something that we have believed.

What belief is driving this question?

What do I think God says about this belief?

For you, knowing that you are not alone in your beliefs or questions is the

2nd <u>Step</u> to finding answers and healing.

thy kingdom come, thy will be done, on earth as it is in heaven.

Who is in the Bible that may have had a similar belief or situation?

- *Why do I relate to him/her?*

- *Where was he/she from?*

- *What was his/her nature?*

What do the scriptures say about this belief?

Scripture reference:

_____

_____

Scripture reference:

_____

_____

Scripture reference:

_____

_____

Now that I know what scripture says about this belief, is my belief a truth or is it a lie?

_____

_____

_____

_____

_____

_____

_____

_____

_____

_____

_____

_____

_____

For you, seeking out and living in the truth is the <u>3rd Step</u> to finding answers and healing.

Give us this day our daily bread.

What do I believe scripture says about my specific question or subject?

Scripture reference:

_____

_____

Scripture reference:

_____

_____

Scripture reference:

_____

_____

What do these scriptures tell me about this question or subject?

 **For you, recognizing the answers that God has given you through scripture is the 4th Step to finding answers and healing.**

And forgive us our debts, as we forgive our debtors

What answers have I found so far?

How does my trust in scripture show up in my day-to-day, concerning this question or subject?

How does my trust in the belief show up in my day-to-day?

What thoughts may I need to change, so I can trust and live within God's truth more?

What answers have I gotten from what I have learned about my belief and God's word?

What needs to change in my answer-finding process the next time I have a question?

What other references could I use to help me find answers?

Although our relationship with God, Jesus, and the Holy Spirit should always be the first step in finding answers, seeking truth, finding healing, and moving on. Having people in our lives who care about our walk with Christ is vital to our healing from our beliefs and questions. People will do this by encouraging us to seek out God's truths/answers and holding us accountable for walking with Him. Again, pray to God for discernment when it comes to opening up to the right people.

Who is my support group to help me stay on the path of finding TRUTH answers?

Mile 5

For you, putting your understanding of God's truth into action in your life is the 5ᵗʰ <u>Step</u> to finding answers and healing.

And lead us not into temptation; but deliver us from evil.

What is my action plan that will lead me to live a day of healing from my beliefs and finding answers?

1.

2.

3.

Who are "my people" that will help me stay on track with healing?

Identify 2-3 people that you will be able to reach out to. It is vital to have more than one so that we do not overload our friends who are dealing with their own burdens. See Ecclesiastes 4:12, "Though one may be overpowered, two can defend themselves. A cord of three strands is not quickly broken."

1.

2.

3.

For you, daily self-reflection along with seeking scripture regularly is necessary. This is the 6th Step.

For thine is the kingdom, and the power, and the glory, and ever. Amen.

Daily Check-in

How do you feel today and why? (Find one word that describes how you feel.)

Today I believe…

I believe this **because**…

I have believed this **before** when…

I start to think _____ when
I believe this way.

What do I do when I believe this way?

What does scripture say about this belief?

What does scripture say about me?

Because scripture is God's truth, today I choose to believe

_____

_____

_____

_____

_____

_____

_____

Give it to God and Go to Sleep

Tips on Leading a Small Group with following Leader's Guide Questions

I want to pat you on the back today for picking up this workbook and being brave. Whether you are working on this alone or working with a group, it shows you are courageous enough to seek out answers from scripture by bringing out awareness that has been buried deep within and stepping into a new and more wonderful life.

As a group leader/facilitator/coach, you are willing to be vulnerable with your heart in a way that will help others feel comfortable and safe so they too can be vulnerable. Remember, you are loved and valued by God.

This workbook can be used as an individual tool or as a group study together. Whichever you choose. Remember, you are worth every minute that you spend drawing closer to God and starting to heal.

As a group leader myself, I would suggest allowing each member to decide on their particular question. On mile marker 1, start by going over the suggested questions for that week and then members work through their questions at home. When you return together the next week discuss any insights or awareness that came up during the week of study and then work through questions for mile marker 2 before ending that night of group time.

Part of the leader/facilitator/coach's responsibility is to make sure that the group feels safe in opening their hearts and thoughts to the group. Creating a safe place for open and honest relationships will build a bond that God rejoices over. You can do this by setting clear guidelines at the beginning of each group time that state things such as….

❖ We are here to love and honor each other

❖ We will never share what was said in this group with those outside the group

❖ We will always respect each other's thoughts and not try to fix the other person

❖ We will be open about our thoughts and feelings

Leading a small group can be so rewarding, yet somewhat intimidating. Here are some things that I've learned over the years.

❖ You will never 100% satisfy everyone

❖ A group will look to you to lead. You can ask for suggestions, but ultimately you will have to make the decisions.

❖ Some in the group may not be comfortable in small groups that they don't know, some are more comfortable in large groups where they can "hide", some like to talk, and some don't. Regardless of how you do your setting, they will engage, or they won't. So, strive for the whole and not the majority or minority.

❖ Be courageous in it. Be brave in challenging your group members. Be bold and vulnerable in your talk. You do these things and the Holy Spirit will be right there with you and God will bless your efforts.

❖ Make eye contact with those who are less apt to speak up. This will let them know that you see them and give them the courage to be open

❖ If in a large group, then set up for small groups. Allow time for large group discussion but add in at least 15 mins of small group discussion on a particular subject for the night.

- ❖ Before the group starts, ask someone to pray. They may not offer but when asked they just may take you up on it, particularly if you're going to use the prayer out of the study guide that your class is using.

- ❖ Be aware of the body language of your audience such as facial expressions. It's okay, if you notice something, to ask them about it.

- ❖ Once someone has said something, you might try either repeating back and/or asking a direct question concerning something they said. This encourages them to speak more.

- ❖ Strive to listen 70% of the time and speak 30%. This may not always work but working towards that will make you more aware if you need to allow more time for the participants to speak.

As the leader/facilitator/coach, we are there for our group. Yes, we will also learn and grow through the process. Understanding how people learn will be your greatest strength and superpower as a leader. There are 3 learning styles: Auditory, Visual, and Kinesthetic. Auditory learners, learn by hearing. So, keep the conversation moving. There is great power in learning from other people's experiences, the wisdom of the group will shine bright and bring awareness to the surface. Visual learners learn from seeing. Be creative but do not overdo it with too many slide presentations, mix it up. You can do this by providing handouts, doing a couple of silent worksheet activities, and then having the group share together, or flip chart group activities. Take some time to think about what would get your thinking processes moving. Kinesthetic learners love to be hands-on. It is all about touch and textures. I love using play doe and having my group create a figure that means something to them. You can google anything, so do some research and get your creative leader/facilitator/coach juices flowing. I know you can do it!

People also learn best and are more likely to remember what they learned by making it personal. There is a style of leading a group called the "Experiential Education Cycle." With whatever subject you are discussing, by using this method you and your group will put what you are learning into practice, changing lives. See the diagram below:

Concrete Experience
(doing / having an experience)
What?

Kolb's Cycle of Experiential Learning

Active Experimentation
(planning / trying out what you have learned)
Now What?

Reflective Observation
(reviewing / reflecting on the experience)
So What?

Abstract Conceptualisation
(concluding / learning from the experience)

Rhonda Gould Coaching & Consulting

Mile 1

Questions for discussion with the group or on your own.

1. Why do you think it is important to identify why this question has come up in your life?

2. Why is it important to know "how" finding the answer would impact your life?

3. How do you think understanding your belief system might help you find answers?

4. Now that you understand what is going on with you, how might it help to know what God thinks about it?

Prayer:

Questions for discussion with the group or on your own.

1. How important is it for you to know you are not alone in what you are going through? Why?

2. Which do you prefer, talking to someone with the exact experience or just knowing that someone has a similar experience?

3. Who, in your circle, do you turn to for support? Why?

4. When you have a belief about yourself or a situation, where do you go to understand that belief? Why?

Prayer:

Questions for discussion with the group or on your own.

1. How important is scripture to your day-to-day life?

2. What is it about scripture that helps you understand your reality?

3. How do you believe God speaks to you?

4. If God speaks to you through scripture, how do you process that scripture?

Prayer:

Questions for discussion with the group or on your own.

1. What have you found out about yourself and scripture at this point?

2. How is it helpful to be aware of how my actions day-to-day come out because of my belief?

3. How does knowing God's truth in scripture, help you?

4. What have I needed to change?

5. What resources have I was not aware of?

Prayer:

Questions for discussion with the group or on your own.

1. Why do you think putting action behind the words is helpful?

2. How do you determine if a person is a safe person to talk with?

3. What are examples of how having a safe person in your life has helped you?

4. How has confiding in someone that was not safe affected you?

Prayer:

Mile 6

Questions for discussion with the group or on your own.

1. How are you about spending time reflecting on yourself and your actions?

2. When scripture is placed in front of you, how often do you reflect on how it pertains to you?

3. What do you believe is the "ideal" time that you spend in scripture a day?

4. What is your process of making sure you spend time in scripture daily?

5. What do you believe God wants from you most?

6. What changes do you need to make to ensure you have time with God daily?

Prayer:

Questions to consider before moving into your process.

1. How might it help you to know or understand that Jesus himself dealt with the same things or types of things you deal with?

2. How important is prayer in your life?

3. How much time do you spend in prayer?

4. What is a redemptive story that God has played out in your life?

5. What is the difference in the roles that God, Jesus, and the Holy Spirit play in your life?

Prayer:

Resources

There have been many books that have helped me in my walk to understanding scripture better, understanding God's love for me, and guided me to live a full and peace-filled life. Although I do not walk this life perfectly all the time. I have learned to give myself grace. I would like to take a moment to share those with you.

Boundaries by Cloud and Townsend

Safe People by Cloud and Townsend

Celebration of Disciplines by Richard Foster

One Thousand Gifts by Ann Voskamp

Braving the Wilderness by Brene' Brown

Power of TED by David Emerald

The Critical Journey by Janet O Hagberg & Robert A Guelich

How to Read the Bible for all it is worth by Gordon D Fee & Douglas Stuart

Effective Group Coaching by Jennifer J. Britton

Atlas of the Heart by Brene' Brown

Just
Breathe

Rhonda Gould   **Coaching & Consulting**

www.ingramcontent.com/pod-product-compliance
Lightning Source LLC
Chambersburg PA
CBHW081537120626
46550CB00009B/2759